How to Swear Like an Elizabethan in Devon

Todd Gray

The Mint Press

For Richard O'Neill, who first expanded my knowledge of English vernacular words and terms.

Cover Illustration: Etching after Pieter Brueghel, by kind permission of Rijksmuseum (RP-P-OB-2394)

The woodcuts have been taken from Charles Hindley, *The Roxburghe Ballads (1873-4)*, in two volumes

ISBN 978 1 903356 68 5

The Mint Press,
Taddyforde House South,
Taddyforde Estate,
New North Road,
Exeter EX4 4AT

Distribution through **Stevensbooks**:
www.stevensbooks.co.uk
sales@themintpress.co.uk 01392 459760

Text and Cover design: Topics – The Creative Partnership, Exeter. www.topicsdesign.co.uk

Printed and bound in Great Britain by Short Run Press Ltd, Exeter.

Introduction

Swearing, cursing and insulting language in Devon, as elsewhere, were part and parcel of everyday life. Blasphemous and insulting words were theoretically prohibited, and thus potentially punishable in court, but most name-calling was probably ignored or discounted. However, many of the examples cited here have come from instances in which a Devonian objected to what had been said of him or her. Their language was generally like that used across England but there were some words and phrases which were atypical such as 'ninnycock'. Whereas many modern insulting terms refer to one of three body parts, many Elizabethan insults concerned misbehaviour. Sexual insults predominated, particularly those alleging illicit acts, and there were over 200 adjectives teamed with the term 'whore'. Accusations of drunkenness, low intelligence, thievery, witchcraft and disease were common. Women were called scolds, men were named as fools and both genders were told they were sexually wayward. These and all the other words in this booklet were used by Devonians to insult, demean or ridicule other Devonians.

The 206 words and terms that have been gathered here caused the greatest offence in Devon at this time, many used in conjunction with others. They here been drawn from original records held at the Devon Heritage Centre and it is likely that some readers will be surprised by the terminology. It is also possible some individuals might be offended at the coarseness of the language but few cannot anticipate that a book on swearing could not have obscenities. No effort has been made to censor the terminology in any regard. The quotations have been reproduced as they were written five centuries ago. The documents that have been consulted are mostly Elizabethan but some also cover the following decades on the assumption that some of the terms recorded in the early 1600s were spoken earlier. A definition follows the entry for each term generally with a Devon example of the original wording in which it once caused offence. A fuller context can be found in *Strumpets & Ninnycocks*, a companion volume.

Thou art a
great arse
whore

Ape an imitator or mimic, as was said in Exeter to describe a man as *'a whoreson ape'*

Arse one's posterior, as referred to in Dawlish when Nicole Tozer was called *'a great arse whore'*, at Dartmouth Ricarda Bream was called *'an Open-Arsed Whore'*, as used in South Tawton when Nathaniel Arscot said of the aptly-named Mary Hole that she was *'a Maggot-Arsed Whore'*, at Bideford when Mary Short was called *'a Squirt-Arse Whore'*, or at Totnes when Joan Knight told Reverend Hill *'Kiss my arse - do as my smock does'*

Ass a donkey, often used alongside the term 'fool' such as at Werrington when one man called another *'a Proud Ass and Fool'*

Bag to impregnate, as when Thomasine Downe of East Down was *'bagged'* by John Pyne

Baggage when used about a man it signifies a worthless or vile man, such as at Exeter when Andrew Bellamy was called *'a Baggage Knave'*, it also signifies a licentious woman, such as when spoken about a Chawleigh woman who was *'a very baggage and may be the occasion of murder'* whereas a Stoke Canon woman was called *'a baggage to ten men'*

Bally rag a contemptible person who is verbally abusive, as used in Cheriton Bishop of the parson who was described as *'a Pilled Rag, Bally Rag'* and *'a Pilled Priest Scabbard'*

Base generally morally despicable but also an illegitimate child

Bastard a child born out of wedlock, such as when said of Barbara Holland of Bradworthy who had two *'bastards sucking at her breast'*, of Elizabeth Warren of Nymet Rowland who was told *'thou hast done so much to have a hundred bastards'* or of Rebecca Jones, of Barnstaple, who was called a bastard who had *'come out of the spawn or seed of a whore'*.

Bastard bearer a woman who gives birth to an illegitimate child

Bastard maker a man or woman that has a child out of wedlock, such as the Tiverton man who was told he was *'a bastard maker and hadest a base child or bastard upon London way which is now eight years old'*

Bawd a man or woman who procures women for their sexual services, such as was said of Maude Lichendon of Barnstaple who *'had been as often times a bawd as there were sands in the sea'* or of Margery Strawbridge of Newton Abbot who was told she was *'an old bawd and thou has two whores to they daughters'*

Beefeater a well-fed menial, as was said of an Exeter constable

Beetle-browed having bushy and overhanging eyebrows, as expressed in Silverton of Elizabeth Facey that she was an *'Old Beetle-Browed Whore'*. It was similar to Joan Bennet at Kentisbeare being called *'a **Black-Browed** Whore'*

Beggar a poor person who asks for financial help, as in South Molton when Wilmot Smith was called *'a Beggarly Whore'*

Bitch and **Bitchery** — a lewd woman, such as when Margery Hardy of Berry Pomeroy was called *'a Bottle-Nose Bitch'* or when an Ugborough woman was called *'a Bitchery and a Baggage'* ; also in relation to female canines such as was said of Agnes Knowling *'you have been as common as a dog and a bitch'* or of a Honiton woman *'many hang about thee as a sot bitch hath dogs'*

Blink-eyed — one who blinks or winks, such as when the parson of Drewsteignton was called *'a Blink-eye and Fucking Priest'*

Blockhead — an utterly stupid man, as the clerk of Yarnscombe was described or at Stratton in North Cornwall where a husband was called a *'blockhead'* for allowing another man to sleep with his wife

Bobtail — a lewd woman, as in Kenton where Elizabeth Goss was called *'a Bobtail and Thievish whore'*

Boobily — stupid, as when Richard Gervis was called *'a Boobily Knave'* in Exeter

Bollocks — testicles, as in Tiverton when William Dodge was told he had the French Pox for which he was given *'oil to anoint thy bollocks'*, of John Pitt also of Tiverton who had sex with Thomasine Frost the consequence of which *'hath beaten away the hair of his bollocks about thy arse'*, or at Stokenham where Robert Knight claimed of Margaret Sprat *'he hath been so far in her as he may go for his bollocks'*

Bottle — in the shape of a bottle, that is round, used variously including when Margery Hardy of Berry Pomeroy was called *'a Bottle-Nose Bitch'* or when Mary Cowte of Stoke Gabriel was told she was *'a Bottle-Arsed Jade'*

Bowl-eyed presumably having eyes the shape or size of a bowl, as used in Totnes of a woman as *'a Bowl-Eyed Whore'*

Breech the backside, as when Joan Deyment of Tiverton was called *'a Fat Breech'*

Bulged a man or woman who has a social disease

Bull referring to a man, as when said in Exeter of a woman that she was *'a Bulled Bitch'*

Bull Beef the todger of a cuckold, as when one man in Exeter's prison taunted another by asking if he had any *'Bull Beef'* to sell

Bull Dog undetermined meaning, said of an Exeter man who was asked *'How now, bulldog?'*

Bull Head a stupid man or blockhead, such as when Richard Gervis of Exeter was called *'a Cuckold and a Bull Head'*, as was Richard Downe of Bideford

Burned or **burnt** a man or woman carrying a social disease, such as William Trickey of Exeter who was told *'thou was burned by a kinswoman of Elizabeth Wills and thou hast now no prick left by reason of the pox and burning'*, it was said in Brampford Speke *'his wife so bad as a bored sow for she burned half an inch of William Myste's member'*, and Elizabeth Forbes of Barnstaple was told *'thou art cursed out of the church for burning John Witheridge his prick and guts… she was the last woman that the said Witheridge did commit the act with or fuck or occupy and that she was as hot as all the ovens in the town'*; with variants ***Burned Tailed*** and ***Burned Arsed***

Thou art a
Cuckold and
a Bull Head

By the Mass blasphemous invoking of the sacrament of the Eucharist, as said in Plymouth *'By the Mass I called her whore and I will call her whore and she is an arrant whore and so I will call her in the pulpit of Plymouth'*

Calf a dolt or a stupid man

Carriage sexual intercourse, as said in Crediton to a woman *'thou art Robert Lane's whore and Henry Harris his whore and they have had the carriage of thee'*

Carrion someone who is vile or corrupt, as when an Exeter woman was called *'Foggy Carrion' and 'Dame Carrion'*

Catchpole an abusive term for a petty officer of justice, as used in Exeter when a man named constables *'Knaves, Rogues, Drunkards and Catchpoles'*

Chatter-Faced possibly Chitty-Faced meaning a thin and pinched face, as was said in Exeter of Rebecca Collins

Cock Leg presumably a reference to a male lifting his leg to urinate, as when said in Exeter that a man was *'a Cock Leg'*

Cockscomb a conceited fool or fop, such as when the parson of St Sidwell's parish was called *'a Fool and a Cockscomb'*

Cod's Head a stupid man but also a scrotum, as was said of John Newcombe in Exeter

Cormorant an insatiably greedy person, such as when Nicholas Pottle of Totnes was called *'a Villain and Cormorant'*

Cozening thieving, as was said of Helen Hooper of Exminster when she was called *'a Cozening Whore and a Slocking Whore'*

Crook Leg a man or woman with misshaped legs, as when Nicole Toser of Dawlish was called *'a Crook-Legged Whore'* as well as *'a Blabber-Legged Whore'*

Crow Porridge vomit, as was said of Thomasine Lyle in Exeter that she was *'a Crow Porridge Whore'*

Cuckold a man who has an unfaithful wife, as was said in Dartington *'thou art a cuckold and Thomas Eliot did make thee a cuckold coming from Newton Bushel'*; Popularly said to have horns as in Cullompton when a man was told *'thou art a cuckold, go in and look in a glass and see how thine horns do grow, heap thy door higher with thy horns'*

Cucumber a cuckold, as when Thomas Fleshman of Tavistock was said that he *'lieth like a cucumber'*

Cunt as now, a woman's private parts, used in Combe Martin when Mary Melhuish was told *'thou hast a cunt like a mare'* or at Colyton when Joan Sincock complained that her neighbour had her taxes reduced she said *'if that my cunt had been as good as Joan Dodge's I had not paid so much to the rate'*; synonyms that were not recorded for Devon, but commonly in national use not long afterwards, include a Black Joke, Bottomless Pit, Dumb Glutton, Madge, Man Trap, Miss Laycock, Money, Mother Of All Saints, Mother Of All Souls, Muff, Notch, Old Hat, Old Ling and Ware

Curtal a lewd woman, as when Amy Smith of Totnes was called *'a Curtal Whore'*

Cutpurse or Cutpocket a pickpocket, as when Margaret Madgent of Exeter was called *'a Tinker's Whore, a Cutpurse Whore and a Thievish Whore'*

Devil such as when said that *'all the devils were in Denbury'*

Dissembling a hypocrite or deceiver, as when a Cockington man was called *'a Old Dissembling Judas'* or when an Exeter constable was called *'a Dissembling Knave Scab'*

Drab a sexually licentious woman, as when it was said of a Littlehempston woman that she was an *'Old Whore and Dribble-Tail Drab and Joan Stink'* or when a Shebbear woman was called *'a Copper-Nosed Drab'*

Drunkard as when a Silverton woman was told *'thou art a drunkard and a drunken woman & wert so drunk at Lammas Fair last at Exeter that thou didst spew or piss about the room or chamber where thou wert'* or of Philip

Michelmore of Buckfastleigh *'thou art a drunkard, a common drunkard and thou hast been so drunk that thy privy members hath been taken out'*

Dunghill the pile of human and animal excrement that was often left in open view, used variously as *'Dunghill Slut'* of a woman at Dartmouth

Epicure an unbeliever in an afterlife or in the divine government of the world, as when the parson of Hartland called his congregation *'base epicures'*

Fart as understood today, often used in the expression *'I care not a fart'* but in Exeter a man under arrest threatened *'I'll fart in Mr Mayor's mouth'*, used more imaginatively of Cheriton Bishop's parson who was likened unto a fart *('I know not from whence thou comest, nor whither thou will go')*

Fat as used today, such as when in Tiverton a woman was called *'a **Fat Arse**'* or of the Crediton woman who was told she was *'a Fat Arse Whore'*

Fie used to express disgust or contempt, as used in Stokenham when a man cautioned another *'Fie, for shame'*

Flat-footed as when used of John Rolston of Netherexe that he was *'a Flat-Footed Cuckold'* or of Elizabeth Ferris of Kenton, and also Alice Thomas of Tiverton, that they were *'Flat-Footed Whores'*

Foggy bloated, as when a Tavistock woman was called *'a Foggy Whore' 'by the Queen's days and who so would go into her house and give her two pots of beer might occupy her'*

Fool a man and very occasionally a woman of little intelligence, often said with the term *'Ass'*

Fornicator a man who has sex outside marriage, such as when Richard Benner of Kingsteignton was called *'an old fornicator'*; variant ***Fornication*** as when said in Bishop's Nympton that *'John Thorne and Agnes Clogge did lye together in a bush of the same wood committing fornication together'*

Fuck as understood today, used at Silverton when it was said of Jane Hedgeland that *'Thomas Walter did fuck her against a garden gate and was not so contented but went into a drang between two houses and there had to do with her again'* or at Whimple when it was said of John Slocombe *'thou didst piss in the Widow Till's backside and thou didst show me thy prick and said this prick hath fucked Joan Peck many times';* with variant ***Fuckery***, which was used to describe the vicar at Malborough near Salcombe

Giglet which sometimes meant a giddy girl but also a lewd or wanton woman, either meaning might have been implied when Mary Bligh of Exeter was called *'a Giglet and young thing'* before being told to go home and learn better manners

God's Blood (or ***God's Bones, God's Wounds, God's Heart, God's Nails***, etc.), blasphemous terms commonly used across Devon, such as when a Newton St Cyres man said *'By God's Blood, I think she was asleep when I was in doing with her'*

Goose a silly fool, such as when the wife of Christopher Kelland of Lapford was called *'a Goose'*

Gossip which could mean a godparent, a close friend, either a woman or a man, who spoke maliciously about other people, as said at Alphington by Philip Beard of Katherine Hayne *'she is a whore although she be my Gossip'*

Hackney a term which originally meant a horse and then a carriage for hire, as used when Alice Bartlett of Heavitree was called *'a Hackney Whore'*

Hardhead a blockhead

Harlot an immoral woman or man, such as when said of James Tremlett of Crediton *'What art thou? Thou art but a Harlot, all the county knoweth it that thou hast a bastard, for it is even there at thy nose and it is thine own picture and thine own body.'*

Hobby a lewd woman, as was said of Joan Stapledon of Woolfardisworthy that she was *'a Scurvy Trash, an Arrant Baggage and a Hobby'*

Hornabus a cuckold, as used in Tavistock of a man who was also called *'a Cucumber'*

Horned bearing the horns of a cuckold, used to describe William Kew of Brampford Speke as *'a Horned Cuckold'*

Horner or Hornmaker, a man who makes another man a cuckold

Innocent a person of low intelligence, as when in Burrington Daniel Rowcliff was called *'an Old Fool and Innocent'*

Jack an ill-bred man, such as used in Barnstaple of its vicar who was called *'a Paltry Jack'*

Jackanapes a monkey or an impudent man, as was said in Totnes *'thou art a Knave, an Arrant Knave, a Jackanapes, a Base Fellow, and come here thou Base Priest and cobble my shoes'*

Jade a lewd woman, as when Grace Cann of Huxham was called an *'Ill-Favoured Drooling Jade'*, when Amelia Lavers was termed *'a Scurvy, Trashing Jade'* or when Jane Hutchin was told she was *'a Base Jade'* that *'didst lie three nights with a tinker at the Magdalene'*

Jakes a privy, used when Joan Knowles of Littlehempston was called an *'Old Jakes'*

Jape to have sexual intercourse, as said about a Plymouth woman who *'the Flemings japed for a waistcoat'*, in Chudleigh when another woman was asked *'dost thou remember when that thou did jape for three half pennies?'* or at Dawlish when it was warned that the vicar would *'jape up all your wives and maidens of your parish'*

Knave a deceitful or troublesome rogue, as when said in Exeter *'thou art a Knave and an Arrant Knave for thou hast attempted my chastity and thou wouldst have had the carnal knowledge of my body'*

Lewd wanton, as used in Cheriton Fitzpaine when the curate was found in bed with Anne Stiggans and Elizabeth Hanmer, *'a Very Lewd Strumpet'*

Lickpot originally the first finger, but used in North Tawton of Vicar Sparke who was told *'thou art an alehouse haunter and doest commonly rail in the alehouse. And thou art a liar. Who is a liar but Sparke? You may go to Bow and there lick men's pots'* by which he was called *'a Lickpot'*

Light sexually promiscuous, as said of Ann Ditchett of George Nympton who was *'a woman of Light behaviour and a company keeper at unreasonable times'* or of Agnes O'Neil of Barnstaple who was *'of loose and uncivil behaviour'* with *'a Light and dissolute life and conversation'*

Lubber a clumsy, stupid man, as said of a Winkleigh man who was called *'a Foul-Mouthed Lubber'*

Lusty being pleasant in appearance or having sexual desire, as a Cheriton Bishop man said of his neighbour, *'I am lusty, I will occupy her'*

Mare a derogatory word for a woman associating her with a female horse, as used in Combe Martin when Mary Melhuish was told *'thou art a Mare and thou hast a cunt like a Mare'*

Mary an oath invoking the name of the Virgin Mary, as said in Exeter Cathedral *'yea Mary, said Peeke, if you stand harkening and play the knave with me I will set you by the heels for I am an officer here and therewithal he laid his hand on the said Davie's bosom'*

Maypole a man's organ, as used to describe a man of Great Torrington

Mazed someone who is mentally incompetent, as when John Dearing was called *'a Mazed rogue'* at Cockington

Mell to have sexual intercourse, as used at Fremington where a man *'did carnally Mell with Joan Vishley upon a bench'* or at Crediton where a couple were seen *'Melling together upon a hurdle in the hogs' house'*

Member a man's organ, sometimes referred to as *'Privy Members'*, in Exeter two couples pulled the bed clothes from a newly-married couple and *'said that they would feel where they were wet or dry, and take the man by the Members and did the like unto her'*

Minion a hanger-on or someone kept for sexual favours, as said of Joan Beard that she was Constable Bennett's Minion

Minx a lewd woman or an impudent one, as when said in Exeter *'How now Mistress Minx? Are you she that threw the sheets into the water? I shall pull your nose from your face, you Cuckold Minx'*

Moon calf a simpleton or a deformed animal, as was said in Crediton to one woman *'you are a notable whore and they say you are with child but it may be none of your husband's for ought I know... I think it is a Moon Calf or it may be a Noon Calf.'*

Muddy morally impure, as when in Crediton Elizabeth Gold was called *'a Base, Black, Muddy Whore'*

Natural a dolt or idiot

Nature the physical after effects of sexual intercourse, as said in Otterton of a husband who thought he had come home moments after his wife had had sex with a neighbour, he said he found *'their Nature on a saddle'*

Naughty a sexually wayward woman or man, as described in St Marychurch of a man (*'a Naughty Whoremonger Knave'*) who had admitted that he desired three men's wives and one of their daughters

Ninny in Devon it signified a young child but generally a fool or simpleton

Ninnycock presumably a combination of a fool and a man's organ, said of an Exeter woman that she was *'a Ninnycock whore'*

Ninnyhammer a blockhead, fool or braggard, as used in Tavistock of Alexander Skerret when he was called *'a Cuckold, a Hardhead, a Ninnyhammer and a Wittol'*

Nippy a man's organ, as said by an Exeter councillor to describe his younger brother

Occupy to have sexual intercourse, as when said *'thy daughter who was occupied in the garden by the vicar of Bradworthy and had half a crown of money, a ewe and a lamb for her labour'* or in Witheridge of Christian Trick *'thou art a whore and George Cruss alias Mogford did occupy thee four times in a night and once was in the morning about break of day'*

Over-ridden a woman who has had a surfeit of sexual intercourse, as when Mary Adams of Exeter was called *'an Over-Ridden Jade'* or when Elizabeth Bartram of Cullompton was told she was *'an Over-Ridden Whore'* who *'lettest the boys to ride thee'*

Paddock a contemptible or spiteful person, as said in Cockington of a man that he was *'a Base Rogue, Mazed Rogue and Beggarly Rogue and a Paddock'*

Pander a procurer of women for sex, as when an Exeter woman was called *'a Whore Pander'*

Patch a fool or an ill-natured person, as was said of a Paignton woman that she was *'a Drunken Patch'*

Pickthank a flatterer, as when an Exeter man was called *'a Pickthank slave'*

Pilled bald due to disease or simply being wretched, nearly only said of clerics such as when said in Payhembury *'I care not a fart for the Pilled Priest'*

Platter Face having a round, flat or broad face, as when a Chudleigh woman was called *'a Platter Face and Stewed Whore'*; similar to a woman at Halberton being called *'a **Broad-Faced** Whore'*.

Play Agrimomsie a term of unknown origins, said in Sampford Courtenay, in which a man paid a woman for sex

Pocky or poxy carrying the pox, often used as *'Pocky Whore'*, such as the Stowford woman who was '*a Poxy Whore, thy guts are almost ready burnt in thy tail'* or used as *'Pocky Knave'* or *'Pocky Rogue'* such as the Bishop's Nympton man who was called *'a Pocky Rascal' 'whose hair does pull from thine head with the pox'*

Polecat a lewd woman, such as when said of a Burrington woman that she was *'a Polecat Whore'*

Prick a man's organ, such as used by a man of Upton Pyne to describe why a married woman preferred him to her husband he said *'I have a better prick than*

he', at Brampford Speke a man was said to have *'felt her secret parts and took up her clothes and put forth your prick'* or in Marldon where it was said *'John Commin did show out his prick unto Margaret Jane and did offer her an angel* [a coin] *to occupy her'*

Pricklouse a term of contempt for a tailor and also a parasite which infested male genitalia, such as when said in Totnes it described Nicholas Pottle along with scab, or when an Exeter constable was called *'a Base, Pricklouse Knave'*

Princock a vain, insolent or saucy youngster, possibly similar to Prinklet, as used in Madron in Cornwall

Privates genitals, as when the vicar of Dawlish *'took this deponent in his arms and showed his privates and would have had pleasure of this deponent'* or in Exeter when it was said of Grace Camp that she had *'behaved herself very lewdly and uncivilly with the said Adams of Clyst St George and suffered him to grope and feel her private parts and to put up his hands or hand under her coats & smock & to take them up in a very lewd and uncivil manner'*

Proud desirous of copulation, as said in Hartland of a young man *'thou Proud boy... like a dog driven as thou are'*

Punk a lewd woman, such as said of Elizabeth Berry in Exeter that she was *'a Punk, a Common Punk, a Base Punk and an Over-Ridden Punk and a Whore and thy child is a bastard begotten by a gentleman in a green satin suit'*

Quean a wanton woman, such as said of Sarah Perriam of Ottery St Mary who was described as *'a Very Idle and Misliving Wench and a Quean as it is thought'*

Ram beggar a poor person, as said of Elizabeth Searle in Exeter who was called *'a Ram Beggar Whore'*

Ram's Mutton a cuckold's wife who was available for sex, as when a man asked another in an Exeter Prison if he could purchase a quarter of Ram's Mutton

Rascal a dishonest man or woman, as used in Topsham of a man *'as rascally a Knave as any within the town'*

Ray hood the hood worn in Exeter to signify a prostitute

Renegade an apostate or someone who deserts or betrays, such as was said of an Exeter man who was *'a Rascal, a Rogue, a Knave, a Renegade and by God's Blood, thou are an Old Conjuring Knave'*

Reprobate unredeemed sinners, as when a Talaton man was called *'a Reprobate Rogue'*

Ride sexually positioning, as used of women such as at Salcombe (*'didst ride upon Owen Bebel's back'*), at Paignton (*'thou dost ride upon every man's back'*) and Broadclyst (*'the boys… were ready to ride on the said Margery's back'*)

Rogue a disreputable man or sometimes a woman, as when it described a Winkleigh man as *'a Thong-Cutting Rogue who committed fornication with the old woman Duke against the door'*

Runagate also **Runabout** a deserter or vagabond, as used in Salcombe of Catherine Small who was described as *'a Runagate*or **Runaway** *whore'* and told *'thou layest with a Frenchman forty times'*

Sard — to have sexual intercourse, as said of a Chudleigh woman *'thou art like unto the woman that did Sard for a bushel of beans and peas' or of a Poughill man 'Milton did sard her in that bed'*

Savage — either wild or cruel and brutal, said of a woman from Rewe that she was *'a Savage Whore'*

Scab — a blood seeking parasite, such as when a Chudleigh man admitted *'I have lain with my dame whiles my master Francis Shapter was cutting out of a course of work and she hath filled me full of the Scabs'*

Scabbard — a diseased person

Scabbed — diseased, as in Totnes when Joan Savery was called *'Mistress Scabbed Arse and Scabbed-Arse whore'* or in Milton Dameral when Edmund Townsend was called *'a Scurvy, Ragged, Scabbed, Pocky Constable'*

Scale-faced — having a skin disease, as when a Bishopsteignton woman was told she was *'a Balled Whore, a Stewed Whore, a Black-Mouthed Whore and a Scale-Faced Whore'*

Scalled — another word for Scabbed

Scold — a woman who persistently railed against her neighbours, as was said in Throwleigh when a woman was told *'thou art an Over-Scold whereby thou wilt undo thy husband'*

Scorpit — a mocking person, used in Filleigh church when one woman asked another *'shall a Scorpit sit in the seat with me, I scorn to have such a Scorpit to sit with me'*

Scum a wretch, as used in Totnes and Exeter to describe women as *'the Scum of the country'* or of a Cullompton woman who was told she was *'a Scum Whore'*

Scurvy carrying disease particularly skin marks, as when Mary Gest of Bovey Tracey was called *'a Scurvy Whore Trash'*

Shaft a man's organ, as when used of an Exeter boy who *'did again draw the pig by his hinder parts unto him and had his Shaft out & drew the pig as near to him as he could'*

Shit as understood today, such as when the rector of Dodbrooke was called *'a Shit Breech Knave'*, of a Dartmouth woman who was described as *'a Shitten Whore'*, of a Chudleigh woman who was *'a Shitten-Heeled Whore'*, of the dean of Exeter Cathedral who was told *'go shit'* and of the diocesan chancellor who was informed *'you will make shit, Sir Reverence, worse than wax'*

Sinkard possibly Stinkard, one who smells, as was said in Totnes to Ann Amyatt *'thou art a Curtal and a Sinkard'*

Sir Reverence this term had three meanings. It could mean 'excrement' or used as an apology similar to 'begging your pardon'. Either of these might have been intended when an Exeter man warned a church official *'You will make shit, Sir Reverence, worse than wax'*. It was also in this sense that an Exeter man said to another he *'did not care, Sir Reverence, a turd for him'*. It was also an ancient custom and in the eighteenth century it was explained in Grose's Classical Dictionary that it *'obliges any person easing himself near the highway or foot path, on the word[s Sir]* *reverence being given him by a passenger, to take off his hat with his teeth, and without moving from his station to throw it over his head, by which it frequently falls into the excrement; this was considered as a punishment for the breach of delicacy. A person refusing to obey this law, might be pushed backwards'.*

Skinning a Mare a couple having sexual intercourse, such as in Tamerton Foliot when Anne Luxmoore and John Parker *'Skinned a Mare together'* or in Kenton when it was said *'a Mare was Skinned down in Mr Hobb's broom close'*

Slave a contemptuous man, as in North Huish when a man was called *'a Vile Slave'*

Slock to take by stealth, as was said of the North Tawton cleric who was told *'thou didst skulk to my house in my absence and did Slock away my goods'*

Slut a dirty woman or a lewd one, or both, such as when in Sandford Joan Clark was said to be *'a Slut no better than a Whore'* or when Joan Deyment of Tiverton was called *'a Brazen–Faced Slut'*

Sot a drunkard or a fool, as was said in Honiton *'thou art a Hot Whore, a Bulled Whore & a Sot Whore & thou hast as many hang about thee as a Sot Bitch hath dogs'*

Stews a brothel or a lewd woman, as used in Totnes when a man was asked *'whether he would live in a Stews all his days of his life?'* or as said of another Totnes woman *'thou art a Stews and thou keepest a back chamber for those men whose wives want meat & can't eat meat at home the whiles'*

Stinking intensive disgust or an offending smell, such as the man in Exeter Cathedral who was told he was *'a Scurvy, Stinking, Proud Fellow'* or of another Exeter woman that she was *'a Filthy, Stinking Whore'*

Strumpet a lewd woman, as used in Great Torrington (*'a Filthy Strumpet'*), Cheriton Fitzpaine (*'a Very Lewd Strumpet'*), Tamerton Foliot (*'a Common Strumpet'*) or Ottery St Mary (*'a Strumpet Whore'*)

Swive to have carnal knowledge, as used in Totnes by *'drunken Burleigh'* who said that the Earl of Leicester had swived Queen Elizabeth

Tail posterior or a man's organ, as was said in Topsham *'thou art an Arrant Whore and thou will have more Knaves pulled from thy Tail'*, at Dittisham it was said of Elizabeth Sharpham that she *'was a Common Whore and that she came after every Knave's Tail'* and at Crediton a man was told he was a Whoremaster who *'hast the Pox in thy Tail'*

Tarse a man's organ, as said in Crediton that William Halston was an *'Old Knave, Old Harlot and Horse Tarse'*

Totter-legged unsteady, as when Sarah Triggs of St Sidwell's parish was called *'a Totter-Legged Whore'*

Trash a worthless or disreputable person, as said of a Plymouth woman who was *'called her Jade, Trash and many others'* or of a Bradworthy woman that she was *'a Scurvy Trash'*

Trull a licentious woman, as was said in Dartmouth of Agnes Wood that she was *'a Drunkard, a Whore, a Drunken Whore and a Trull Baggage'*

Thou is
a Very Lewd
Strumpet!

Turd as understood today, used in Silverton when a woman was told that she was *'a Haggle-Tooth Whore and that she was so well known that within ten miles of her no man would set a Turd'*, as said of an Exeter churchman *'I care not a Dog's Turd for you'* and as told to another cleric *'a Turd in your teeth'*

Varlet a dishonest man or one of a low disposition, as was said of a man in Down St Mary that he was *'a man of small honesty or credit and a Common Varlet and tale bearer and no credit to be given unto him'*

Villain an unprincipled scoundrel, as was said of an Exeter man that he was *'a Villain Knave'* or a Pilton man was *'a Naughty Villain'*

Ware a man's organ, such as said in Marldon when John Commin offered his *'Ware'* to Margaret Jane

Wench a young woman, as was said in Cullompton when a man admitted he was *'here playing with a pretty Wench'* or at East Down where it was asked *'did you hear anything of John Bussacott? He lay with a Wench in Molton and drawn so much in her tail as if he had thrown a bucket of water after it would have been a horse colt'*

White Hare a term with an unknown meaning, a woman of Broadclyst was described as *'a White Hare with two legs'*

White Toad another unknown term which was used, along with *'Whore Pander'*, to describe an Exeter woman

Whore the most common insult given to Elizabethan women to suggest they were sexually wayward, as was said of Jane Hobbs in Plymouth *'thou art a Whore, an Arrant Whore and thou dwellest in a whore*

house'. Many women were identified with the place in which they were active including Broom Close Whore, Ditch Whore, Furse Whore and Hedge Whore. Some women were called Old Whores whereas others were called Cunning, Filthy, Foul, Muddy, Notorious, Ragged, Ratted, Rotten, Scurvy, Stinking or Ugly Whores. There were a number of more inventive terms:

Bald-arse, possibly Balled Arse, as when in Colaton Raleigh the wife of Richard Howe was called *'a Bald Arse Whore'*

Black-faced, as when a woman of Kentisbeare was called *'a Black-Faced Whore'*, which may have been similar to when Susan Mills was called *'a **Black Whore**'* in Exeter and another Exeter woman was called *'a **Black-Mouthed Whore**'*

Chamber Pot, referring to the practice of women in brothels who held a chamber pot for their clients, as said in Lapford when Anne Rennet was told '*thou art a Base Whore, Chamber Pot Whore and that thou didst hold the chamber pot to Philip Crispen and George Bellamy*', which may have been the same when a woman of Berry Pomeroy was called *'a **Piss Pot Whore**'*

Copper-Nosed, from the practice of treating syphilis with copper and the use of artificial noses to correct nose disfigurement and loss, as when Alice Rowland was called in Shebbear *'a Copper-Nosed Whore'*

Full of Lice, covered with parasites, as when a woman of Welcombe was called *'a Full of Lice Whore'*

Thou art
an Arrant Whore
Maker Knave as any
in Devonshire

Gouty-Legged, encumbered by gout, as said in Totnes of Wilmot French that she was *'a Gouty-Legged Whore'*

Hollow-Mouthed, possibly indicating a lack of teeth, as said of Alice James in Shebbear that she was *'an Arrant Hollow-Mouthed Whore'*

Long-Nosed, as was said in Shobrooke that Judith Scorch was *'a Thievish Whore and a Long-Nosed Whore'*

Tallow-Faced, having a pale or yellowish complexion, as when Agnes Cox of Widworthy was called *'a Whore and a Tallow-Faced Whore'*

Whore maker a man who converts a woman to whoredom, as said in Drewsteignton *'thou art an Arrant Whore-Maker Knave as any in Devonshire'*

Whoremaster a procurer or pimp, as was said in Ilsington *'there was not such an Old Whoremaster more in the country and said that there was not such a Bawdy Old Knave in the country'*

Whoremonger a fornicator or lecher, such as used in Crediton (*'thou art a Whoremonger and thou had'st Palmer's maid behind the door in a new year's day in the morning'*), Staverton (*'thou art an Arrant Whoremonger and thou hast a hundred whores and thou wilt have them if they wore white kerchiefs upon their heads'*), Chudleigh (*'thou art an Arrant Whoremonger and thou didst call forth Isabel Spark from the dance and didst offer her 12d to occupy her'*) and Rackenford (*'thou art a Whoremonger and thou has had the parson's wife in thy chamber and the doors shut upon thee and there didst hug her and kiss her, and thou hast had to do with the Foulest Whore in the parish, and one that lived by the alms of the parish'*)

Whoreson the son of a whore, as used in Spreyton (*'Whoreson Priest'*), Exeter (*'Whoreson Cuckold'*), and Berrynarbor (*'Whoreson Drunkard'*)

Witch said of both women and men to imply dealings with Satan, as was said in Crediton to Wilmot Basse *'thou art an arrant Old Whore Witch, thou hast almost witched thine own eyes out... I could find it in my heart to fry thee in thine own grease'*

Wittol a husband who was complicit in his wife's adultery, the term was often described in Devon as being *'nine times worse than a cuckold'*

Woodcock a dupe or fool, as used of one Kingsbridge man as *'a Rogue, Rascal and Woodcock'*

Wren's Nest a woman's pubic hair, as said in Ottery St Mary when Thomas Follett put his hand upon Margaret Crispen's French bodice and *'did put his hand a little further and catched her by the Wren's Nest and pulled away some of the hairs'*

Yard a man's organ, as when a Kenton man said to a passing woman *'I have a thing here Mary may do thee good, holding his Yard in his hand and making water'* or said of a Sheldon man who *'was swollen in the Yard as big as a tinning pot which would hold three pints'* and was *'as black as the bottom of a pot'*